B. P. Pratten

The Egyptian Difficulty and the First Step Out of It

B. P. Pratten

The Egyptian Difficulty and the First Step Out of It

ISBN/EAN: 9783337244330

Printed in Europe, USA, Canada, Australia, Japan

Cover: Foto ©ninafisch / pixelio.de

More available books at **www.hansebooks.com**

THE
EGYPTIAN DIFFICULTY

AND THE

FIRST STEP OUT OF IT.

LONDON:
P. S. KING & SON, PARLIAMENTARY AGENCY,
CANADA BUILDING, KING STREET, WESTMINSTER, S.W.
1884.

Price Sixpence.

THE
EGYPTIAN DIFFICULTY

AND THE

FIRST STEP OUT OF IT.

I.

The Egyptian difficulty, as it now stands—although the historian or the political philosopher may trace it back as far as his love of research may lead him—practically dates, so far as Europe is concerned, from the final collapse of the rule of Ismail, rather more than five years ago.

The problem then before the Powers especially interested in Egypt was relatively simple and easy of solution. Nevertheless, the difficulty not only exists to-day in as acute a form as ever, but it agitates, with increasing intensity, the whole political surface of Europe, producing a situation fruitful in embarrassment and pregnant with danger.

It is curious to look back over these five years, and to observe how disproportioned to the intrinsic complexity of the problem which presented itself for solution in 1879, is the mass of extraneous political tangle which has since overgrown it.

Such retrospect discovers the military revolt in Egypt as the first consequence of the solution adopted for the original problem, and it was speedily followed by the naval demonstration and the massacres in the Delta. This last brought the problem fairly before Europe; and then followed in rapid succession the Conference of Constantinople, the bombardment of Alexandria, the war against Arabi, the mission of Lord Dufferin, the British attempts at administrative reorganisation, the disaster of Teb, the mission to Abyssinia, the avenging expedition of General Graham, the mission of General Gordon, the Conference of London, and lastly, the mission of Lord Northbrook and the Nile expedition under Lord Wolseley.

One after another, the several schemes included in this long tale of experiments—save only the last-named pair, of which the outcome has yet to be seen —have each in their turn proved sterile or abortive. Not one of them has made any impression on the difficulty, while their collective result has been the aggravation of its involvement, and the general worsening of the outlook. And what a list it is! What a round of conference, mission, and war; war, mission, and conference, all to no purpose.

History has never before recorded so brave a show of grand, costly, and sanguinary futility.

Nor is it possible to survey this astounding array of failure without suspecting that there must have been a bad beginning, a false start, that the solution of 1879 had in it an original sin which vitiated whatever virtue it might have contained, and of which the perpetuation, marring every experiment, has brought to nought the conferences, missions, and wars lavished upon the patching up of what was in reality a hopelessly bad job from the outset.

The purpose of these pages is to show that such original sin did exist in the solution of 1879; that the sequence of failures which we have recapitulated above has been mainly caused by that sin; that so long as its taint is suffered to remain in the mass under treatment, the conferences, missions, and wars of the future, or whatever other devices the ingenuity of statesmanship may imagine, will fail like those of the past. Finally, we hope to show that it may be eradicated.

How stood the case in the month of June, 1879?

The showy imposture of the reign of Ismail was played out; the tinsel of it was stripped off; the cruelty and the sham of it were mercilessly revealed. It was known to those Powers who were called upon to deal with the case, that the power and prestige of the Khediviate had greatly suffered in the last days of Ismail's reign, nor were indications wanting that his exactions, his reckless financing, and the foreign intervention resulting from it, had created discontent which was already "gnawing the bowels of the commonwealth," and would have openly declared itself but for Ismail's watchfulness and energy.

The problem therefore which then presented itself for solution was to find a successor for Ismail, in whom the power and prestige of the Khediviate should be revived; a man untainted by the odium of the previous reign, acceptable to the population, and with energy and tact to quench, or at least to contain, the smouldering fires of discontent lighted by the tyranny and trickery which had impoverished the population and brought Egypt to bankruptcy.

Such was the problem; and the Powers interested sought to solve it. But how? By the enthronement of a lay-figure provided with a custodian at either elbow to shape its postures. And these custodians were rivals, forbidden by the force of circumstances from pulling their wires in unison.

No particle of prestige attended Mehemed Tewfik to his throne. All the pretty things that were said about him in foreign newspapers, when he received his Firman of investiture, only provoked a smile in Egypt; and the meaning in that smile soon found other forms of expression.

But even surrounded as he was by the ruin, the discontent, and the odium which were his royal inheritance, the "amiable young prince" might yet have proved innocuous with one firm and wisely guiding hand on his shoulder to keep him in the way he should go. For although all Egypt knew full well the nullity of his mind and character, he had not at that time grown personally obnoxious to the population.

This chance, however, was denied to him. In the cross-pulling of the dual control, and the ferment of the national movement, he quickly became distracted, and hopelessly committed himself in the eyes of the population. In his flurry and bewilderment he proved to be anything but innocuous; his vacillation, weakness and feeble craft precipitated the crisis of 1882, and added greatly to its intensity.

By this time the Khedive Tewfik had become irretrievably obnoxious to the Egyptian people, and consequently worthless, and impossible, thenceforward, as an instrument for any of the purposes of administrative or social reconstruction.

II.

When England came in force upon the field of Egypt, she did so as the champion of order and of the political state of which the Khedive, as legal ruler, was the personification. There was no time then, nor was it the season, to look into details. The programme of England was to suppress the revolt, and to reinstate the Khedive upon his throne. This, with the ample resources at England's command, was the work of a few weeks.

But although it proved to be no herculean labour to re-enthrone the lay figure which was the lawful Khedive, yet, when the image of authority was restored to its niche, it was quite another thing to animate it with the spirit of the authority it symbolised. To reorganise the administration, to revive the power which had crumbled to dust in Tewfik's own hands, was, with Tewfik again on the throne, a task upon the difficulty of which the victors at Tel-el-Kebir had not calculated.

What appeared to be the leprous limb of the Egyptian body-politic had been amputated, and the English fondly imagined that a tonic regime would now restore the whole system to soundness. It was soon, however, their lot to discover that the disease was in the body rather than in the severed member. They had got rid of the one only element that showed vigour and unity of purpose, and when they found themselves left with Tewfik upon their hands, in a chaos of disorder and dissension, they came to doubt whether they had taken the better part, and were driven to seek for consolation in the purity of the abstract principle upon which the course of their action was shaped.

It might reasonably have been expected that so soon as this principle had been vindicated, the very first thing done would have been carefully to scrutinize the efficiency of the instrument through which the English were about to begin their work of reorganisation. But no such idea apparently ever crossed the British mind. Having restored the Khedive, whoever he might happened to have been, to his throne, it certainly became the right as well as the duty of England, to consider whether Tewfik who happened to be that Khedive, was the fit man for the Khediviate. And the duty of so doing was all the more obvious as those very events which had called forth British action, afforded a very strong presumption that he was not.

However, the British having spent their blood and their money on putting Tewfik back in the place he had been too weak to hold, there Tewfik was to remain; and notwithstanding his proved weakness, and the contempt and aversion of the Egyptians, Tewfik was to be imposed upon Egypt as its future ruler at all hazards.

That this was the precise formula in which the British decision was shaped, we do not pretend to say. All novel-readers know that when the hero of the tale plunges into the stream, and rescues the drowning maiden from the torrent, he straightway falls in love with her and marries her. If she happens to be blind, or half-witted, or hump-backed, it only adds to the charm of the romance.

The British are the most chivalrous and, consequently, the most gentle-hearted people in the world, and they were precisely in the position of the hero of the tale. In the process of delivering Tewfik from his peril, there sprang up in the natural generosity of the British mind a feeling of personal interest in the creature they had saved. The deliverers began to find their hearts warming with tenderness towards the man they had rescued; they came to regard his defects with compassionate indulgence, to look upon him as "their man," and then, *more Britannico,* to stand up for him. Ultimately, even, they were almost ready to persuade themselves that they were under obligations to him, as was seen by the replies to Lord Randolph Churchill's accusations against Tewfik in the House of Commons.

With all our respect and admiration for British chivalry we are bound to say that, on this occasion, it was singularly misplaced. The English might have lost sight of the fact that the sacrifices of men and money which their country had made, were not for the sake of the man, but for that of the principle of which he chanced to be the embodiment. But it seems strange, to say the least of it, that they should have forgotten that it was through his egregious incapacity that the necessity for these sacrifices had arisen.

As to England being under obligations to Tewfik, the idea is pure absurdity. To the "amiable young prince" the appearance of the troops upon the scene was salvation. Death stared him in the face. His personal safety, the recovery of his shattered authority, everything, in fact, depended upon British assistance. All he desired to do was to throw himself into the arms of his deliverers. He had, moreover, neither the imagination to conceive, nor the energy to follow, any other course.

In this confusion of misapplied principle and misplaced sentimentality, the English have never practically recognised the impossibility of building up a strong administration in Egypt with Tewfik at its head. They would have had a better chance of doing so even with his father; for although Ismail, hated and discredited quite as much as his son, could never again acquire any hold upon the national mind, he has both the dexterity and the energy to keep a firm grip upon the national body. Tewfik cannot boast of these endowments.

But although we may find a more or less satisfactory explanation of the British infatuation for Tewfik, in its early existence, it is inexplicable that disenchantment did not swiftly follow when the order was given to the army, under Hicks Pasha, to advance upon Obeidah against the Mahdi. We have no reason or right to expect wisdom or statesmanship from Tewfik; but here was a case when he might, by deference to British opinion, have shown that he was at least capable of perceiving an opportunity of showing his gratitude.

The opinion of Lord Dufferin regarding the Soudan was perfectly well known to Tewfik; no imperative emergency forced his hand; Khartoum was safe while Hicks and his army remained there. And yet, with the advice of Lord Dufferin fresh in his memory, Tewfik committed the gratuitous and disastrous blunder of sending Hicks and his army to destruction. It is no excuse for him that he was incapable of forming an opinion upon what he was about. Given his intellectual calibre, he may, indeed, be excused for not having learnt by experience to distrust his own feeble judgment. But it is wholly inexcusable that, knowing the opinion of Lord Dufferin on so great a matter, he should have set that opinion at defiance.

It is needless here to recapitulate the disastrous

effects of this act of supreme foolishness. It points straight enough to the original sin of the solution of 1879, perpetuated because it pleased the English to make a toy of their own out of the broken puppet of the dual control.

III.

A somewhat closer inspection of the intellect, temperament and character of the prince, whose nomination as Khedive was the fatal flaw in the attempted solution of the Egyptian problem in 1879, is here due to our readers, whom, however, we may reassure by stating that we have no intention of leading them in a dreary pilgrimage through all the events of his reign. Neither is it of our purpose to heap abuse upon the head of a man who has failed simply because he has not in him the stuff of which success is made. All our design is to show that the insuccess of Tewfik in the past is due to natural defects; that to the dead weight of these defects are now added the dislike and contempt of the Egyptian people, the distrust of the sovereign government, and the abhorrence of all that is influential in Islam.

Let it then be admitted that Tewfik was placed in a position of singular difficulty, and that there are many more who, in such a position, would have succumbed to its difficulties, than would have proved themselves able to cope with them.

But beyond suggesting that Tewfik is a more fit object for pity than for blame, what else does this teach? It teaches that misgovernment even in so small a country as Egypt, with its primitive and docile population, may lead to complications of almost inextricable involvement; that difficulties having once arisen in Egypt it is necessary to recognise in this fact a forewarning of what may occur again; and that a man whose gifts are far below average, is not a fit occupant for the throne of Egypt, more especially when he is further weighted by the dislike, distrust and contempt of every element, political and social, whose support and confidence could give stability to his throne.

With the "amiability" of the young Khedive, of which Mr. Mackenzie Wallace speaks with a very visible shoulder-shrug, we have no concern. Tewfik's organisation is of a low type. His intelligence is small, and he has no single element of force in his constitution. He lacks courage, energy, will, resolve, and principle. At the same time he is not free from the spirit of intrigue, characteristic of the stock of his grandfather Ibrahim Pasha, and prominent in his father, in his late uncle, in one, at least, of his brothers, and in other members of the family branch whose names it is unnecessary to bring before the public.

This feature in his character was displayed in early manhood, when he tried to place himself at the head of a puritan moslem party to contrast with the ultra-European ways of his father, then on the throne. The idea was not his own; it may fairly be doubted whether he was capable of conceiving it—his " abilities are too infant-like for doing much alone." It was suggested to him by a foreign adventurer, who had courted and failed to captivate the fancy of Ismail, and who has long since disappeared from the Egyptian scene. But if Tewfik did not originate the idea, he dropped kindly into the scheme, which suited his predilections; and for a brief space the "party" existed. The Khedive Ismail, however, soon found it out; took prompt measures to disperse it, sent the busy foreigner out of the land, and took Prince Tewfik into the Cabinet, as Minister of the Interior, to keep him at once out of the mischief that Satan finds for idle hands, and under the vigilance of his paternal eye.

This is an old story, but even so long ago as the date of it the doctors of Islam had little faith in Tewfik, with all his sanctimonious ways, and his ready quotations from the Koran. Many, indeed, of his own party—especially after the Khedive found it out—condemned him for intriguing against his father. And, apropos of this distrust of the Mahommedan teachers, we remember the impression he produced upon a very great light of Mecca, who after his accession came to Cairo to ask a favour of him. Tewfik welcomed the venerable Sheikh with many old " odd ends stolen forth of holy writ," and much parade of Koranic lore, and his visitor obtained from him all he had come to ask. But when he was leaving the presence, he expressed to his suite in very brief and emphatic terms his measure of Tewfik's intelligence, and the last word of his verdict was "hypocrite." This dictum went the round of El Azhar, and was long the talk of the learned Mahommedan clique of Cairo. How often has it not, since then, been quoted!

That Tewfik played the part of Louis XIII. to the Richelieu of Riaz, the evidence is too strong to allow of any doubt. So far as his abilities permitted, he favoured the schemes of the National party in order to deliver himself from the dictation and overbearance of his minister. But when he had attained his end, he proved too weak and incapable to lead the National party, and threw himself into the arms of Sir E. Malet. Then he sought to excuse himself to the National party by pleading the impossibility of resisting the pressure which England brought to bear upon him.

Thus flitting like the bat in the fable, and fluttering like a scared bird, Tewfik's conduct through the crisis of 1881-2 was a weak parody of his father's vacillation in the last days of his reign. But in the case of Ismail, through all the vacillating period, there were signs of will, of purpose, of resource—though the bad faith was too glaring for purpose to live, or for will to have effect; while with Tewfik there were neither will nor purpose, but only feebleness and shuffle, till at last he dropped *nolens volens* upon the bosom of England, where he found asylum, because there was no other refuge.

Too much obscurity overhangs what passed between Tewfik and the National party after Tel-el-Kebir, for us to make any use in these pages of the statements current on the subject. But whatever may have been the real facts, they have left upon the Mahommedan mind an impression at once so deplorable and so indelible, that as a ruler of a Mahommedan people, Tewfik is impossible.

To resume, Tewfik is too slenderly gifted in point of intellect to take a clear view of any position in which he may be placed, and too infirm of purpose to follow out any line of conduct with consistency. His duplicity may be a symptom of weakness only, and not of moral obliquity. Be it so : let us regard it as the unconscious tripping of a man who either does not know his own mind, or has none to know. But this has practically nothing to do with the question. Doubtless there is much to be said in extenuation of Tewfik's shortcomings. But our concern is with the shortcomings themselves, with the consequences of them, with the position they have created for Tewfik in national opinion, and, above all, with the impossibility, owing to that position, of making any good use of him in the reconstruction of the shattered government of his country.

It has been urged, and on Tewfik's behalf, that, for the purposes of reorganisation in Egypt under British guidance, a passive Khedive is required. There may be some truth in this. But if the passive Khedive is surrounded by an active popular hate, his mere presence, however absolute may be his passivity, acquires an active force. Moreover, to be nothing but a dummy requires a certain amount of *vis inertiæ*, and even this negative form of strength Tewfik has shown that he does not possess.

It has been said that Tewfik is odious to his subjects and to Islam at large, because he is the creature of England. It would be much nearer the truth to say that the English are obnoxious to Egypt and to Islam, because they have adopted Tewfik as their creature.

IV.

Great are the expectations raised by the mission of Lord Northbrook, and nowhere has it caused hope to bound higher than in Egypt. Jaded with the wear of tyranny and the rack of disorder, the people are fain to discover in the very name of Northbrook a distant resemblance to an Arab word signifying "good luck," and to take comfort in the smile even of so pale an omen. They know, moreover, that Lord Northbrook besides being a Cabinet Minister, is a tried and successful administrator, and that he won his laurels as such among Eastern peoples. There is every justification for their hopes. May they be realised to the full!

But the mission of Lord Northbrook can only result in advantage in so far as it may lead, in the first place, to the practical recognition of the facts to which, in the preceding chapters, we have drawn attention; thence to a true appreciation of them; and, onwards, to conclusions in harmony with their significance and importance.

Whatever the conclusions may be, they must inevitably contemplate one of two alternatives, viz: either the more or less prolonged exercise of British influence in Egypt, or its withdrawal.

To the disinterested spectator of the events of the last two years it appears impossible that, for any continuance, a Power so Great as England, and owing so much of that greatness to moral prestige, should consent, or rather submit, to cut so poor a figure in Egypt as England has done during that period. It is not only that the moral prestige and dignity of the British Empire directly suffer from so distressing an exhibition of insuccess, but the condition of affairs resulting from the infirmity of the British position in Egypt emits, so to say, an irritating vapour, heavily charged with mischief, which pervades the whole Eastern hemisphere.

This acrid exhalation frets the Egyptians themselves, and dries up the germs of confidence; it hardens their hearts against the English and prejudices them against English measures; it encourages intrigue and fosters the restless spirit which has been rife in Egypt since the abortive solution of 1879; it has increased the moral corruption in the country, it has called new ambitions into play, and imparted new fire to others which, if not extinct, had subsided into latency.

In England it tends to debilitate the government, and is as the breath of life to its political opponents.

It keeps France on the *qui vive*, inspires the press with matter for satire and objurgation, it sours the feeling between the French and British people, and imperils the good understanding between the two governments.

It is welcome to the nostrils of the Porte, and soothes the wounded self-love of the Turks, but it does this at the expense of England, and nourishes a spirit adverse to the establishment of that agreement on Egyptian affairs, which, as we shall presently show, is so eminently desirable.

Its suggestive inspiration renders the other States of Europe impatient, and also stimulates them to seek their opportunity in the embarrassment of England, suggesting the application of an obvious leverage, which operates a painful strain upon British diplomacy throughout Europe.

It permeates India, and tends to engender ideas which from the British point of view, at least, must be regarded as eminently unwholesome.

That all this is presently injurious, and that it is heavily fraught with future danger, our readers will be ready to concede.

If, then, England is to continue, for a while, to exercise a direct influence in Egypt, it is absolutely necessary that her position in that country should be fortified—not by more soldiers or more cannon, but by sympathy and confidence. But before there can be any real fortifying, the principal element of moral weakness—the main source of antipathy and distrust—must be extirpated.

Moreover the only thing that can justify the prolonged stay of England in Egypt is the prompt and masterly reconstruction of the administration, and this is impossible while the main pivot of the administrative mechanism is so weak as to preclude its endurance of even the ordinary vibrations of the machinery revolving upon it.

Unless the British are able to form a strong administration in which the native population shall cheerfully acquiesce, and in which the Powers of Europe shall recognise an ample promise of stability, their further sojourn in Egypt has no *raison d'être.* It can only aggravate the evils already multiplying in the country, irritate Europe, and prove to England a fruitful source of trouble, danger and humiliation.

But if England cannot keep her hand upon Egypt without forming an administration of unquestionable efficacy, worthy of herself, and apt, as it then would be, to inspire the Egyptian people and the Powers of Europe with confidence, it is still more impossible that she should quit Egypt until this has been effected.

To do so would not only be a cruel and crushing satire upon all the blood-spilling of the last two years, but, inasmuch as it would deliver up the country to anarchy and violence, it would, also, be an outrage against humanity.

The responsibilities which England has assumed

in Egypt have been too solemnly undertaken to be dropped because their first-fruits prove thorny in her grasp. Nor, if it came to the point, is there any one Power that would be willing to share them, nor any, except possibly Turkey, that would be willing to assume alone the burden of them.

Thus, whether Lord Northbrook comes to the conclusion that it is desirable that the exercise of direct British influence in Egypt should continue or should cease, the practical result is the same. That is to say, England can neither remain in Egypt without forming a strong administration, nor quit Egypt without first doing so.

It is not our business here to hold up to notice the weak point in the British cuirass which this dilemma reveals. Of course there remains a *pars tertia*: England might cry *Peccavi!* and, laying her sorrows at the feet of the Powers of Europe, might invoke their benevolent commiseration, entreat them to let her go home, and to do with Egypt whatever their superior strength and wisdom might suggest. But we may pass over this *reductio ad absurdum* of the question, and proceed.

With the brilliant example of India before their eyes none can doubt but that England is fully capable of establishing a strong British administration in Egypt. But the hands of the British Government are tied against so doing by their respect for the existing political order, and by the repeated declarations repudiating the idea of either protectorate or annexation, which that respect has dictated. In her present difficulty England is, doubtless, to a great extent the victim of the delicacy of her political conscience. But the fact that the situation is of her own election rather increases than diminishes the obligations attaching to it.

As the result, then, of her own free choice, England is bound to do the work of administrative reconstruction through the instrumentality of an Egyptian government, conformable with existing firmans and with the political state created by them. And inasmuch as it was for the maintenance of this order of things that the British army fought at Tel-el-Kebir, the attitude of the British Government in abjuring any disturbance of it is logical, loyal and consistent.

To what point then in our argument do these considerations bring us?

England has practically no choice as regards staying in Egypt or leaving it; she cannot consistently assume a protectorate over the country, nor annex it. Staying, the obligations of her own greatness, going, the still greater obligations of humanity, impose upon her the constitution of a strong government. And this government she is pledged to construct out of materials which, if they are not to be found in the actual corporeal substance of the existing order, shall yet be in all respects of the same character, consonant with the principle of the order, and compatible with its maintenance.

Now, it has been shown in what precedes that the most important factor in the present composition of the existing order is bad, effete and unimprovable. Therefore the first step towards reconstruction is the elimination of what is rotten, and the substitution for it of new material possessing the requisite soundness and tonicity.

V.

We now come to another point which has a very important bearing upon the reconstruction of the administration in Egypt. In carrying out this work it is necessary to include in it every possible provision for its efficiency, and to surround it by every precaution for its preservation, so that it may be exposed to the fewest possible disturbing influences, and may combine as many as possible of the elements necessary to secure the tranquillity of the country.

We believe it to be impracticable to ensure the perfect tranquillity of Egypt without previously securing the goodwill of the Porte, because the Imperial Government possesses almost inexhaustible means of disturbing it, and of maintaining a constant under-current of adverse influence, for the promotion of which there will never be any lack of efficient instruments, so long as Constantinople is willing to employ them and to pay for their services.

While Tewfik is on the throne it is absolutely certain that this will be the case.

Tewfik is for many reasons in the worst possible odour at Yildiz. In the first place: all that has been distasteful to the Sultan, in the course of recent events, is attributed to him. Secondly: he is the one tangible object that impersonates the difference between the relations of Egypt with the Porte in the past and in the present. Thirdly: he has entirely lost touch of Moslem sympathy. Fourthly: he has neglected the forms and usages of vassalage, or, what is worse, he has performed them in so tactless and irregular a fashion as to make a series of affronts out of what should have been courtesies.

As regards the first of these reasons for the disfavour with which Tewfik is viewed, no explanation is needed. Just as the Egyptian people have arrived at the conclusion that Tewfik is an utterly incapable ruler, the Sultan and his Ministers have, although by a different path, been led to a similar conviction.

The difference between the past and present relations of the Porte with Egypt cannot be defined in a sentence; nevertheless there is a very perceptible difference, which, to a sovereign so highly sensitive as Abdul Hamid, is extremely galling. The Khedive, in the past reign, came to pay homage to the Sultan; presents were sent, and the aviaries and other *vivaria* of the imperial establishments were replenished with choice specimens of the *fauna* of Central Africa; a regular correspondence was kept up between Egypt and the Porte: the *Kapou Kehaya*, or agent of the Khedive at the Porte, was assiduous in showing attentions at the palace; and although there was no actual exercise of sovereign power, the sense of it was always kept alive, and the Sultan felt himself to be sovereign of his dependency. All this has been cut off; and even if Tewfik had the tact and ingenuity to attempt to revive it, which he has not, the ill-will borne to him is now too deep for him to have any chance of success.

It is a yet more serious difficulty that Tewfik should so entirely have lost touch of Moslem sympathies. The policy of Abdul Hamid is to cultivate these sympathies to the utmost; he pursues it with marked ostentation, and his whole heart is set upon it. By no possibility, then, could the Sultan feel complacency in the rule of Tewfik in Egypt; and the Moslem Sheikhs of Egypt and the Hedjaz, to whom Tewfik is *anathema maranatha*, will always have his Majesty's ear and his entire sympathy.

There is one token of deferential respect which no vassal prince, or governor-general, ever omits, and that is to send to the Sultan on four occasions in every year—viz., the Bairam, the Kourban-Bairam, the day of the Sovereign's accession, and his birthday, a telegram of congratulation. This is the irreducible minimum of deferential show expected by the Sovereign from the vassal. Albeit, the two latter have not in all cases the same importance as the two former. But for a Moslem vassal to neglect, on either of the two great festivals of Islam, to send his message of homage to the Khalif, is an unpardonable slight. No message came from Tewfik to the Sultan either on the Bairam or Kourban-Bairam of last year. After the second omission the Grand Vizier wrote to Tewfik to expostulate, and the answer was that he was so much occupied about the cholera that he "forgot it." To "forget" to salute the Khalif on such solemn occasions is the worst form of *lèse majesté*. At the last Bairam, Tewfik sent a most effusive message to the Sultan; but it was so exaggerated in its terms, that when it was contrasted with the previous omissions, it was simply set down to apprehensions on account of the break-up of the London Conference a few days before, and was regarded as a clumsy attempt to make his peace with the Sultan, in a moment of misgiving as regards the stability of his own position.

All these things we have deemed it necessary to explain, in order to show that the antipathy of the Sultan to Tewfik rests upon grounds which preclude any possibility of reconciliation.

Therefore, while Tewfik remains on the throne of Egypt the sovereign government will always encourage intrigues against him; and whatever importance, relatively speaking, British opinion may attach to these intrigues, they will always have a disturbing influence, will detract from the efficiency of the administration, and, more or less, jeopardise the maintenance of tranquillity.

If Tewfik were a man of any power in himself, or if there were any imperative reason, from a British point of view, why Tewfik, and no one else, should occupy the Egyptian throne, it might be resolved to make the best of the hostility of the sovereign government, and counteract it by all available means. But, on the one hand, Tewfik is not a man of power, and the intrigues of Stamboul would inevitably lead him to a repetition of past blunders. On the other, there is no imperative reason, from a British point of view, why he should be maintained on the throne. Among the many reasons why he should not, there is one of which, though for different reasons, England would, no less than the Sultan, recognise the validity, viz. : that he has lost the confidence of the Moslem population. It is obviously not England's policy to add to her burdens by giving gratuitous offence to Moslem feeling.

The action of England in Egypt, although in actual fact it does not overstep the limit of the powers and privileges granted by Imperial firman to the vassal province, and does not therefore infringe upon the sovereign rights of the Sultan—merely supplying the deficiencies in the vassal government—nevertheless obscures those rights. This is a source of grievous irritation at Yildiz, and frets perpetually the wounded *amour-propre* of the Sultan. It is this which leads the Porte to harp upon the point of the evacuation of Egypt by the British troops. The obvious fact that evacuation is impracticable has no weight with the Porte; and thus a vicious circle is created which renders it impossible to bring England and Turkey to an understanding.

There is only one mode by which this vicious circle can be broken.

The Sultan desires that Tewfik should be removed,

for reasons which have already been fully explained. He also desires that the obscurity in which events have shrouded his sovereignty should be dispelled, and that he should stand before the world, in the strong and unequivocal light of an act of unmistakable significance, as the Sovereign of Egypt.

If, then, England were to suggest to the Sultan the fitness of deposing the Khedive, and of appointing a new Viceroy in his place, there can be little doubt but that the Sultan would discern in the proposal the opportunity of realising both his desires at one stroke. Tewfik would be removed, and, in presence of a firman under the hand of Abdul-Hamid, deposing him and appointing his successor, there could be no longer any doubt who was Sovereign of Egypt.

Thus the *amour-propre* of the sovereign government would receive a brilliant satisfaction; and at the same time England would be rid of the main obstacle to the construction of a strong administration in Egypt. The source of Turkish ill-will having been removed, there would be no longer anything to fear from Turkish intrigues working against British endeavours to establish and maintain tranquillity in the country.

VI.

The conviction that the exigencies of the situation require the removal of Tewfik from the Khedivial throne immediately suggests the consideration of the question of a successor. The maintenance of the existing order, to which England is pledged, demands that there shall be a Khedive in Egypt nominated by the Sultan.

It may reasonably be presumed that the Sultan would, in his choice, be as conservative as the circumstances would allow; and whether or not his Majesty deemed it necessary to respect the firmans of 1866 and 1873, which altered the line of succession in favour of the late Khedive's children, and which cost Egypt £150,000 a-year and the bondholders untold sums, he would at all events be unwilling to disturb the settlement of 1841, which vested the viceroyalty of Egypt in the family of Mehemet Ali.

To propose to alter the provisions of the settlement of 1841 would be to open a very wide question; and if the landmarks it affords were shifted at one point, there is no practical limit to the changes that might ensue.

It is, therefore, improbable that the Sultan would wish to disturb the settlement of 1841, which is the basis of the existing order, as by doing so he would virtually release England from her pledge to maintain that order.

England, bound by her pledge, could not consistently put forward a candidate whose election would not be compatible with the maintenance of the settlement of 1841.; and, moreover, unless the British Government were prepared to assume a protectorate, they would not care to open the way to the many difficulties which a disturbance of that settlement would call into existence.

It lies, therefore, beyond the purpose of these pages to discuss the fitness of a new political construction for Egypt, such as would necessarily result from any derangement of the settlement of 1841. We shall, therefore, confine our search for a new Khedive amongst the members of the family of Mehemet Ali, to whose descendents that settlement assured the Egyptian throne.

There are several members of this family whose claims to the throne may be considered. They are (1) Ismail Pasha, the late Khedive. (2) Abbas Pasha, the infant son of Tewfik. (3) Halim Pasha, the only surviving son of Mehemet Ali. (4) Hussein Pasha, son of Ismail Pasha. (5) Hassan Pasha, also a son of the late Khedive.

(1) The reappointment of Ismail Pasha has been much mooted latterly in the continental press, and His Highness has been very active in bringing his claims before the European Courts and before the public.

The first objection to his restoration seems to be the self-stultification which would attend his acceptance by the Powers who, five years ago, insisted on his removal. But this is not in itself an insuperable objection; if the Powers saw fit to stultify their action of 1879, they would not be materially the worse.

Another objection, more serious, is, that the restoration of Ismail would not be acceptable at Yildiz, and it is exceedingly doubtful whether the Sultan could be brought to agree to it. With regard to this point, however, it must be said that Ismail Pasha is a great adept at manipulating the wires of opinion in Constantinople; and, when it is remembered what, backed by the ample purse which confiding bondholders were good enough to fill for him periodically, were his achievements in this way during his reign, and, also, how considerable is the fortune he carried away with him from Egypt, no one, least of all Ismail himself, would despair of reconverting Turkish opinion to his side. Such, indeed, is his own firm conviction, and his agents in Constantinople are only waiting for the master's signal to proceed on the old lines.

It must not, at the same time, be forgotten that the prejudice against Ismail at Yildiz, originates in the vituperative attacks upon the Khalifate in Arabic and Turkish newspapers published in Europe, which the Porte believes to have been patronised and subsidized by him. This offence it would take a flood of gold to obliterate.

But it is nevertheless necessary to consider what would be his chances of succeeding in Egypt on a second trial.

Ismail Pasha is far from being a common-place man. He is well-informed, knows Egypt well, has great energy, and is remarkably wide-awake. He has an inexhaustible imagination, and ideas breed in his brain as rapidly as animalculæ in water. Though no administrator he is a strong despot, and knows well the use of the iron rod. He is a genius in his way; but his genius is peculiar and erratic, and his moral character is dominated by the vivacity of his imagination.

The return of Ismail Pasha to Egypt would not be welcome to the country. It was during his reign that were sown those seeds of discontent, of which the development has caused all the woes of the last five years, and in this melancholy process the hatred of Ismail has become rooted in the Egyptian mind. If he were restored to the throne he would not be able to use the means by which during his reign he maintained his supremacy; and, considering this change of conditions and the confirmed dislike of the population, it is very problematic whether he would be able to exhibit his old form as an iron-handed despot—the only form to which he has been trained, and which his nature understands.

It is also necessary to keep plainly in view that one of the first conditions of the establishment of a strong administration in Egypt is the hearty acquiescence in it of the population. This acquiescence would certainly be wanting if Ismail were at its head.

We may fairly give Ismail credit for having

learnt some wisdom by adversity, or at least for having art enough to seem to have done so. The very variegated moral skin which he showed as Khedive may, perhaps, have been shed; but he was always something of a chameleon, and knew how to adapt his tint to the light immediately beating upon him. This art he will not have lost; and too much trust must not be placed in any colour he may show.

Weighing, then, all that may be urged for and against the restoration of Ismail, all that can be said of it is that it would be an experiment of considerable risk, which would not combine two conditions essential to the construction of a strong administration, viz.: the cordial acquiescence of the Egyptian people, and the genuine approbation of the sovereign government, even if this latter were obtained, in form, by means of a pecuniary transaction..

(2) The appointment of Abbas Pasha, the infant son of Tewfik, would involve the necessity of a Regent. This is in itself a complication to be avoided, unless it should prove to be the only possible combination.

The only reason which would recommend such an arrangement is that Abbas, according to the terms of the firmans of 1866 and 1873, which modify the order of succession as established by the firmans of February and June, 1841, is the next heir to the throne.

It may be worth while here to consider what may be the claims of the later firmans to be respected rather than those which they supplanted; whether it is expedient to recognise those claims; whether the later firmans are revocable; and whether they were, at all events as regards the succession, ever strictly legal.

The principal claim of the firmans of 1866 and 1873 to our respect is, that they cost Egypt and Egyptian bondholders a vast sum of money. In consideration of that of 1866 an addition of £150,000 a-year was made to the Egyptian Tribute, and large sums were spent in the purchase of the influence at Constantinople necessary to obtain the Imperial sanction. For the firman of 1873 there was no overt bargain; but a large slice of the Oppenheim loan of that year was expended in procuring it. Having paid so heavily for the dislocation of the order of succession, the country and its creditors may consider that they have a right to the undisturbed enjoyment of what they bought. On the other hand they may be of opinion, looking at the results of their bargain, to which, albeit, they were not privy, that it is not worth while to throw " good money after bad " to keep it in force. We can discover in the firmans of 1866 and 1873 no other claims to respect either moral, material or even technical.

As to the expediency, there would be no question on this point if the next heir were manifestly a desirable person to occupy the throne. But all that can be said on this subject is that for the present he is a nullity, and that what he may be hereafter is a lottery. It certainly would not be easy to find a Regent. Nubar Pasha, the only qualified man whom Egypt furnishes, would not be acceptable either to the country or to the sovereign government because he is an Armenian ; and, if he were appointed, a large proportion of his considerable powers would be engaged in foiling the intrigues that would be directed against him. Such being the case, there would certainly be no obvious expediency in upholding the provisions of the firmans of 1866 and 1873 regarding the change of succession.

The question of the revocability of the firmans referred to may be very easily answered. These firmans are in themselves the revocation of other firmans, and the firman of 1879, appointing Tewfik to the Khediviate, revoked certain of the provisions of those of 1866 and 1873. A multitude of other precedents might be cited to show that firmans are revocable; so that, as regards the abstract right of the Sultan to revoke a firman, there can be no doubt. But to establish the special right in this case we have only to turn to the preamble of that of 1866. This passage in the Imperial rescript recites as follows :—

Ayant pris connaissance de la demande que tu m'as soumise, et dans laquelle tu me fais connaître que la modification de l'ordre de succession * * * * *serait favorable à la bonne administration de l'Egypte, et au développement du bien-être des habitants de cette province:*

This is the one consideration in virtue of which the change of succession was granted in 1866 ; the "good administration of Egypt and the development of the well-being of the inhabitants" was what Ismail engaged to give in exchange for the boon he asked for his family. Neither in his own reign, nor in that of his son, has this engagement been observed. The history of the reigns of Ismail and Tewfik is a grotesque satire upon the preamble of the firman. The non-fulfilment of its prime condition incontestably invalidates it.

And now as to its legality. We venture to think that the firman of 1866 was an immoral transaction. It was not the spontaneous act of the Sultan Abdul Aziz; it was obtained by increasing the Egyptian Tribute. Egypt was at that time already insolvent; so also was Turkey. The Porte required new revenues to pledge for new loans, and in 1871 did pledge this increment of the Egyptian Tribute for a loan of £5,700,000. By this addition Ismail committed his insolvent country to an additional charge upon its already insufficient, and then rapidly diminishing, revenues, in order to obtain an exclusively personal benefit. The persons he dispossessed of their chance of inheritance were not parties to the transaction. Their rights were bought over their heads, on the false pretext stated in the preamble of the firman, with money that did not belong to the purchaser, and the expenditure of which imperilled the financial stability of the country with the government of which he was entrusted, as well as the rights of the bondholders who had lent their money, never dreaming of this new burden upon Egyptian resources. It does not add to the morality of the transaction that vast sums were spent on the purchase of influence in Constantinople in 1866, and that still larger sums were similarly expended in 1873, —all bondholders' money, lent to rescue the country from nancial embarrassment, obtained on that false pretence, and spent for the private advantage of Ismail and his family. Such a transaction contains no element of legality.

We have been led into this digression by the necessity of considering the claims of Abbas, the son of Tewfik, to be appointed Khedive in the event of his father's deposition. The matter we have discussed comprises the only question which bears in any serious sense upon the nomination of that youthful claimant.

(3) It is now the turn of Prince Halim to be considered. Halim Pasha is the youngest and only surviving son of Mehemet Ali. He is an Egyptian; his mother was a Bedouin, and he is now in the prime of manhood. He is the heir to the throne under the provision of the firmans of 1841, and would, in the order of succession secured by those firmans, have succeeded Ismail, but for the immoral traffic of 1866. His record so far as it goes is irreproachable. He is well-educated, high principled, intelligent and manly. Egypt has a favourable remembrance of him, and his friends in the principality are numerous. He might have had a "party" in Egypt had he so chosen; but he has always stood aloof from political intrigue, and although his interest in Egyptian affairs has been deep and vivid, and although he has never had any faith in the Ismail branch of his House, he has

sedulously abstained from presenting himself, ever so modestly, as a pretender. Since he has lived in Constantinople he has been urged to accept office in the Ottoman Cabinet, and once he was persuaded to take a place as Minister without portfolio. But office in Turkey was not compatible with his tastes and inclinations. He is a straight-forward, upright man, of a large and generous nature, and with a stable character that is no slave to the impulse, passion and caprice that distinguish Ismail. He has the gift of inspiring respect; the Sultan highly esteems him, and both in native and foreign circles in Constantinople he has the highest standing. His large establishment, for he is very wealthy, is a model of order, propriety and good taste; in fact he is "every inch a gentleman," and no one who knows him will pronounce any other opinion. Whether he would make a good Khedive is a question that can only be answered by experience. But it may generally be predicated of one who wisely and honourably administers his own affairs, that he will wisely and honourably administer any other affairs that may be committed to his charge; and the man who in private life has the gift of inspiring respect, and grouping friends about him, will exhibit the same gift in public life.

(4 & 5) We may take together the two sons of Ismail, Hussein Pasha and Hassan Pasha. They are a striking contrast to each other. Hussein is quick, clever and prone to intrigue, and has many points of resemblance to his father, who was afraid of him.

Hassan is of the *bon enfant* type, resembling his brother Tewfik, quite as weak as he is, but without the petty cunning which the present Khedive calls to his aid in awkward moments. It is difficult to discover in either of these scions of the Ismail branch of the House of Mehemet Ali, any special qualifications that would recommend them for the Khediviate.

Our list is exhausted. If the settlement of 1841 is to hold good, Prince Halim appears to be indicated as the successor of Prince Tewfik.

VII.

We have now only to resume, as briefly as we may, the substance of our argument and the conclusions to which it points.

For the last five years the affairs of Egypt have sped on a broken wing.

England, involved in them by the force of circumstances, has had to bear all the moral blunt, and much of the material cost, of all that has gone amiss.

The origin of the chequered tale of the last five years lay in a false solution in 1879—the appointment of an incapable ruler, and the institution of the dual control.

The dual control has disappeared; the incapable ruler remains.

It is now necessary to create a strong government in Egypt.

Whatever may be the policy of England, she cannot disconnect herself from the country, any more than she can remain in it, without forming such a government.

This England might do by direct protectorate or by annexation; but the government of England has abjured both of these courses.

The strong government has therefore to be created out of the existing order, or out of the material consonant with it.

There cannot be a strong government with a ruler who is (1) incapable, (2) obnoxious to the people, (3) distrusted by the sovereign government, (4) under the ban of the religion of the country.

(1) Incapable : he will be always liable to fall into dangerous mistakes.

(2) Obnoxious to the people : he will lack the support and sympathy necessary for success.

(3) Distrusted by the sovereign government : he will always be the object of intrigues hailing from Stamboul.

(4) Under the ban of the religion of the country : he will be the constant *irritamentum* of fanatical opposition.

Under such disadvantages, not only is the present ruler a useless instrument for the purposes of administrative reconstruction, but the fact of his presence is prohibitive of any such reconstruction.

His only hold upon his throne being due to the protection of England, all the obloquy attaching to him is reflected upon England.

Under the weight of this obloquy British influence

is discredited; and thus the moral power of England goes to waste in supporting a man who is useless to herself.

Therefore, the "First Step" out of the "Egyptian Difficulty" is to place the present Khedive in retreat, and replace him by some one who is neither (1) incapable, (2) obnoxious to the people of Egypt, (3) distrusted by the sovereign government, nor (4) under the ban of the national religion.

Who this shall be depends upon what firmans are to be upheld and what to be revoked.

There are reasons, which have been shown, why those of 1841 should be upheld.

There are reasons, which have also been shown, why the immoral bargains of 1866 and 1873 should be cancelled.

Working out the problem on these lines, the only man who appears to be eligible for the Egyptian throne—that is to say in whose person the four above-mentioned conditions are combined—is Prince Halim, who also happens to be the lawful heir.

But this is matter for investigation. The question of succession is only brought forward here because the advocate of demolition has no right to be heard if he cannot at least suggest a means of reconstruction.

It is on the demolition that we insist; because the actual structure shuts out all light from Egypt, and condemns the government which has undertaken to guide its destinies, to work in a dark shadow of distrust and antipathy, wherein no plan can ripen and no endeavour fructify.

www.ingramcontent.com/pod-product-compliance
Lightning Source LLC
Chambersburg PA
CBHW030710110426
42739CB00031B/1634